www.providencebooks.net

Publisher Contact

Email:contact@providencebooks.net

Social media: facebook.com/providencebooks

Acknowledgements

The team at Providence Books would like to thank our friends, family, suppliers and customers for making our vision of creating the highest-quality books a reality. Thanks for purchasing and enjoy the quotes!

This page is intentionally left blank

This page is intentionally left blank

A lot of people use social media to share mundane things or for self-glorification. I try to use it to share interesting things with people.

Ashton Kutcher

A lot of the characters I play are very naive, and I don't think I'm like that. And I'm not stupid!

Ashton Kutcher

Acting can be so much fun that it's easy to forget that what you're doing is a job. But if I've got my tie on, I'm going to work.

Ashton Kutcher

After 'Punk'd,' my company Katalyst did a deal with AOL to produce short-form content for the Web. At that time it was a different game. If you got front-page coverage on any popular website, you could probably get a push.

Ashton Kutcher

Always roll up the sleeves on your shirt. It gives the impression that you're working, even if you're not.

Ashton Kutcher

Americans think that they have a history, but it's nothing compared to Europe.

Ashton Kutcher

Anyone who has tried to build something that changes people's lives sometimes finds life to be a distraction, and finds people who don't care as much as they do to be annoying.

Ashton Kutcher

Anyone who wants to be an entrepreneur like someone else is actually looking in the wrong direction. You don't look out for inspiration, you look in. You have to ask yourself how can I be better today, at solving the problem I am trying to solve for my company. I wouldn't encourage anyone to be like me. Just be like you.

Ashton Kutcher

As marriage goes, I think most people sort of set being - you know getting married as the goal as opposed to being married.

Ashton Kutcher

Be careful with the man jewelry. A little goes a long way.

Ashton Kutcher

Don't settle for what life gives you; make life better and build something.

Ashton Kutcher

Entertainment, really, is a dying industry.

Ashton Kutcher

Everybody likes to hold up a really big righteous sword when people make mistakes. Well guess what, now it's recorded and everyone has access to it... so let's stop judging people.

Ashton Kutcher

Everyone loved Steve Jobs and the idea of Steve Jobs. Like a lot of people, I loved a man I never knew.

Ashton Kutcher

For me, the most entertaining evening would be to go sit with entrepreneurs and talk with them about how they're building their companies and how we can help to make them better. That's the one thing in the world - well, I love doing that.

Ashton Kutcher

I actually used to be a front for the largest national sports-betting syndicate in America.

Ashton Kutcher

I am only young once, who cares if I'm a goofball!

Ashton Kutcher

I believe that opportunity looks a lot like hard work.

Ashton Kutcher

I can't grow a mustache. It's pretty sad if I attempt to.

Ashton Kutcher

I certainly don't think I'm deserving of taking up space forever as a human. There's a whole generation of people yet to be born that are going to be so much more evolved than I am. I don't want to take up space. They're going to be better equipped to make the world a better place than I am.

Ashton Kutcher

I could never be with a woman who felt like she needed to change me.

Ashton Kutcher

I could never be with a woman who felt like she needs to change me.

Ashton Kutcher

I definitely believe that if you stop working at relationships, they go away.

Ashton Kutcher

I didn't come from the worst of situations, and I didn't come into the best of situations. But I've appreciated the best situations. And I've made the best of the worst situations. I'm lucky to be where I am.

Ashton Kutcher

I didn't really go the starving-artist route. I kind of went and did massive, commercial things.

Ashton Kutcher

I don't believe that old cliche that good things come to those who wait. I think good things come to those who want something so bad they can't sit still.

Ashton Kutcher

I don't buy these rag magazines that feed off of stolen, you know, press. They're basically stealing someone's image in order to make money for themselves... They wait at the end of my street in their cars. Every time I exit my home, I have company.

Ashton Kutcher

I don't have to act for work anymore; I can act for passion. That's freeing, but it's also a prison of its own. When you can do anything you want, you're really responsible to do something great. And that's scary.

Ashton Kutcher

I don't read the magazines that make things up about people. I know what the truth is. I don't sort of indulge in my own fodder. I don't really care what they write about me.

Ashton Kutcher

I don't think I'm a funny person in general. I have had to learn comedy.

Ashton Kutcher

I don't think opposites attract. I think like attracts like. So I don't think that they do attract, opposites. Only when you're talking about magnetic poles.

Ashton Kutcher

I fail frequently - I just try to keep it quiet.

Ashton Kutcher

I feel like a fraud... My name is not even actually Ashton. Ashton is my middle name.

Ashton Kutcher

I guess I really haven't thought much about winning an Oscar, but if I had the opportunity, I'm sure I would like it.

Ashton Kutcher

I have someone that cooks for me... that's the best thing ever. I just want to show up and I want my house to be like a hotel... so I want to have a couple of options... I like to have a couple of options.

Ashton Kutcher

I learned what a Birkin bag is from the price tag. You'll never forget what it is once you've paid for one.

Ashton Kutcher

I like a high boot on a girl.

Ashton Kutcher

I live my life like anybody else, and people choose to write about mine. And what they write I can't control - when they write lies at least - because the laws can't really protect you unless you can prove malicious intent. So I just choose not to read it.

Ashton Kutcher

I never thought in my life, I never really thought I would get married. I watched my parents go through a divorce, and I thought, like, this is just not something people are supposed to do.

Ashton Kutcher

I really think that technology has the greatest potential to accelerate happiness of most things in the world. The companies that will ultimately do well are the companies that chase happiness. If you find a way to help people find love, or health or friendship, the dollar will chase that.

Ashton Kutcher

I really think that you have to find a partner that compliments you and is somebody that pushes you and is better at some things than you are, so they can push you to improve yourself as a person. That's my take.

Ashton Kutcher

I really think that you have to find a partner that compliments you and is somebody that pushes you and is better at some things than you are, so they can push you to improve yourself as a person.

Ashton Kutcher

I think I probably think about myself as an actor, which is the way most people do. I think I'm good, I don't think I'm great. I think I would hire somebody else to play me in the movie about me.

Ashton Kutcher

I think Ryan Gosling is a really great actor who's meticulous about his work. And I'd love to have the guts that Johnny Depp has to actually go outside the box on a character. When he plays a character, he plays it in a way that nobody else would.

Ashton Kutcher

I think about the automobile, I think about like, when I was a kid, you know, the invention of the answering machine, which I was like, 'Wow.' Or call waiting, which was, like, very big. It was a very big thing. Call waiting was a very big thing. And these incremental innovations happen constantly.

Ashton Kutcher

I think at all social networks, be it Facebook or Twitter or whatever it is, there's an ecosystem that exist there. But there's also an ego system that exists there.

Ashton Kutcher

I think people know Steve Jobs the showman. I think people know the guy who stood up and gave the keynotes. The magician. The salesman.

Ashton Kutcher

I think privacy is valuable. You don't have to share everything, and it's healthy to occasionally hit the pause button and ask yourself if you're oversharing. But at the end of the day, if you're not doing anything wrong, you don't have anything to hide.

Ashton Kutcher

I think that romance sort of coincides with effort, so you can fall flat on your face, but as long as you're making a great effort, I think it comes off as romantic. So it can be something as simple as, like, if you're someone who doesn't cook, you can make a meal.

Ashton Kutcher

I think that the way that Steve Jobs sought after love was to create products that people loved. And when people loved his products, in turn they - he felt like they loved him.

Ashton Kutcher

I think that when we start thought-policing people and idea-policing people, then that's crossing a line. And I think, you know, everybody's so afraid of this imaginary line of thought police that they forget their own personal safety.

Ashton Kutcher

I think we've all been in the middle of doing something we cared about, when someone coming in the room and saying 'hello' was annoying. I personally can understand that, as someone who tries to create.

Ashton Kutcher

I trust my government. I actually have a trust for my government with my data, and I trust them to protect me. They've protected me - they've made the best efforts to protect me my whole life.

Ashton Kutcher

I try to make good decisions as decisions come up.

Ashton Kutcher

I want to be like Tom Cruise from 'The Outsiders' and go on and do amazing movies for a long time.

Ashton Kutcher

I wanted to be a genetic engineer. That was my goal in college. I wanted to figure out what the codon sequence was that causes replication in a cardio myopathic virus. That was my goal.

Ashton Kutcher

I was on Facebook. I was on MySpace. And somebody said to me, You should check out this thing called Twitter. I knew five people that were on it, so I started following those people and seeing what they were doing, and then I applied my own sensibility to it. The more that I shared, the more people started following me.

Ashton Kutcher

I woke up many mornings not knowing what I'd done the night before. I'm amazed I'm not dead.

Ashton Kutcher

I would just like a woman someday, somewhere, at some point in my life to say to me, 'You're a great listener.' Haven't heard it yet, and that's a superior compliment to get from a woman. But I'm going to work on it.

Ashton Kutcher

I would say I'm 90 percent collaborative in everything I do, and 10 percent of the time I just make the call.

Ashton Kutcher

I would say probably my most alpha quality is my competitive nature. I'm very competitive, and it tends to bring out very much the man in me.

Ashton Kutcher

I wouldn't say I'm personally trying to transition from comedy into drama. I don't look at things like, 'Oh, I need to do a drama now.' I get a lot of material sent to me, and if I feel like something has the creative integrity and the right director and the right whoever involved, the right actors and is a great story, then I do it.

Ashton Kutcher

I wouldn't say you have an online life and a real life. I think technology is just mapping and organizing what already exists.

Ashton Kutcher

I'll probably never be the best actor in Hollywood, but I hope to be the hardest working.

Ashton Kutcher

I'm a guy's guy. I don't comb my hair unless I have to, and I don't use lotions or fancy shampoos.

Ashton Kutcher

I'm continually trying to make choices that put me against my own comfort zone. As long as you're uncomfortable, it means you're growing.

Ashton Kutcher

I'm from Iowa, we don't know what cool is!

Ashton Kutcher

I'm happy wherever I go, whatever I do. I'm happy in Iowa, I'm happy here in California.

Ashton Kutcher

I'm not a follower of this or that religious leader. More wars are started because of religious leaders, and people are following and they don't know why... That is religiosity. That is what turns people into robots.

Ashton Kutcher

I'm very awkward when I have time off. I don't know what to do with myself. It's weird not to work.

Ashton Kutcher

I'm very tech-forward. However, I also think hitting the pause button is not a bad thing, and really connecting with people one-to-one viscerally, having a connection with someone, is really important.

Ashton Kutcher

I've already exceeded my expectations for myself. I'm one of the most influential people! I mean come on! I wanted to be... I never thought the things I've experienced in my life, I didn't think that was the life that I was gonna get to live.

Ashton Kutcher

I've constantly done my best to get the best material I can get with the best directors I can get to direct me.

Ashton Kutcher

I've had some really, really wild fun nights in Vegas. I ended up on stage once with this band, The Digital Underground, doing the Humpty Dance.

Ashton Kutcher

I've learned the hard way how valuable privacy is. And I've learned that there are a lot of things in your life that really benefit from being private. And relationships are one of them.

Ashton Kutcher

I've never had a job in my life that I was better than. I was always just lucky to have a job. And every job I had was a steppingstone to my next job, and I never quit my job until I had my next job.

Ashton Kutcher

I've usually found that the greatest rewards in my life come from taking on things that are a little bit scary.

Ashton Kutcher

If Facebook gets your entire social graph, you don't necessarily want to share everything with your entire social graph. You might wanna parse that social graph. So there's a company called PASS that is a private social network that I personally use for my friends and my family.

Ashton Kutcher

If Google decided at any point to publish my search history, or your search history, or anyone's search history, there's a litany of things they could idea police you about, and if it was published, you would be publicly shamed. Everyone would be publicly shamed. But we trust Google, and we trust the people that run that company.

Ashton Kutcher

If you really want to make a relationship work, at some point in time, you're going to have to make some sacrifices and do some things that are a little bit uncomfortable.

Ashton Kutcher

In e-commerce, your prices have to be better because the consumer has to take a leap of faith in your product.

Ashton Kutcher

In the movies, you want a good story and characters that are honest, but you are also looking for a good director who can lead the ship. That's how we look at business. Everybody has a great idea for a start-up, and so do their relatives, and they tell me, 'You gotta build it.' I say, 'I have to believe in it.'

Ashton Kutcher

It's hard to appreciate success in modeling, because it's not something you feel like you've earned, so there is a little bit of bread of shame that comes with that. It's like somebody giving you a puzzle that's already put together.

Ashton Kutcher

It's really easy, once somebody passes away, for the tales about them to become taller, the good ones and the bad ones.

Ashton Kutcher

Katalyst is a merger of three industries. A piece of us is connected to ad agencies. Because we get the complex overlay of the social Web, we know how to engage an audience and how to make entertainment for the social Web. And we know how to gain and activate and retain an audience. So we create social networks for brands.

Ashton Kutcher

Leapfrog innovation - consistent, constant, ridiculous leapfrog innovation - only happens within a dictatorship. Any time you try to do something really innovative, most people aren't going to understand it until after they experience it. So when you're developing in innovation, you have to be a dictator.

Ashton Kutcher

Life can be a lot broader... when you realize one simple thing: And that is that everything around us that we call life was made up by people who were no smarter than you. And you can build your own life that other people can live in. So build a life. Don't live one. Build one. Find your opportunity, and always be sexy.

Ashton Kutcher

Modeling is the best because you have to look hot, which comes easy to me, you know. I'm blessed with that.

Ashton Kutcher

My goal is to embrace the people, the 'natural resources' of Israel, and to build businesses with the creative Israelis.

Ashton Kutcher

My mom is still yelling at me because she needs more autographed pictures.

Ashton Kutcher

My mom's whole side of the family, they're all Packers fans. My mom's a Bears fan. My stepdad is a Vikings guy. So that gets ugly. My mom sits upstairs watching the Bears game; he sits in the basement. They can't watch it together. Football's a violent anger in our family dynamic.

Ashton Kutcher

My parents couldn't give me a whole lot of financial support, but they gave me good genes. My dad is a handsome son-of-a-gun, and my mom is beautiful. And I've definitely been the lucky recipient. So, thank you, Mom and Dad.

Ashton Kutcher

One of the things I've become immune to is people talking about market cap and social media platforms.

Ashton Kutcher

One of the things about being on Twitter, for me, is mostly about just being on the pulse of what people are interested in, what people are doing and what people are looking for. I look at entertainment projects and storytelling, and I really try to think about what people want.

Ashton Kutcher

Opportunity looks a lot like hard work.

Ashton Kutcher

People used to behave morally because they thought God was always watching - in some ways God today is the collective, and the collective is watching.

Ashton Kutcher

Romance is sort of an island right next to care. When you care about someone and you listen to them and you hear them and you can feel them and you know just what's right, and generally it's something that will be very unimpressive to a room of strangers.

Ashton Kutcher

Seriously, women have a level of outward compassion that a lot of men don't necessarily have. Guys feel as deeply as women, but they don't share it as much. Learning how to do that more has been a valuable add.

Ashton Kutcher

Steve Jobs had something like a 90% approval rating from his employees. You hear stories about him being this short-tempered, aggressive person, which he was. But he was in the pursuit of making people around him better, so the product they created would be better.

Ashton Kutcher

Steve Jobs was a pretty complicated character and somewhat a psychologically complicated guy.

Ashton Kutcher

The failures that we have are sometimes expensive educations.

Ashton Kutcher

The film industry brings people together, and so does technology. I see them as similar platforms.

Ashton Kutcher

The goal is not to get into a relationship; the goal is to be in a relationship.

Ashton Kutcher

The power of a handwritten letter is greater than ever. It's personal and deliberate and means more than an e-mail or text ever will. It has a unique scent. It requires deciphering. But, most important, it's flawed.

Ashton Kutcher

The reality is that we communicate with every part of our being, and there are times when we must use it all. When someone needs us, he or she needs all of us. There's no text that can replace a loving touch when someone we love is hurting.

Ashton Kutcher

The scruffier your beard, the sharper you need to dress.

Ashton Kutcher

The sexiest thing in the entire world is being really smart. And being thoughtful and being generous. Everything else is crap. I promise you. It's just crap that people try to sell to you to make you feel like less. So don't buy it. Be smart. Be thoughtful and be generous.

Ashton Kutcher

The sexiest thing in the entire world is being really smart. And being thoughtful. And being generous. Everything else is crap!

Ashton Kutcher

The thing that enchants me the most is the ability women have to feel other people's pain. The total empathy that women have is extraordinary.

Ashton Kutcher

The truth is that I'm an idiot. I am. I don't do things by the rules sometimes. I say things that I probably shouldn't say. I push buttons. I deserve to be made fun of. And I feel like, as soon as you can make fun of something, it instantly removes the fear.

Ashton Kutcher

There are a lot of perks that come with fame, and with every positive there's a negative, and then it all kind of balances out.

Ashton Kutcher

There is some argument about who actually invented text messaging, but I think it's safe to say it was a man. Multiple studies have shown that the average man uses about half as many words per day as women, thus text messaging. It eliminates hellos and goodbyes and cuts right to the chase.

Ashton Kutcher

There was a point in time where I was doing movies to be able to afford to live in a certain way.

Ashton Kutcher

There's no sense in making life seem like it's a struggle, because that doesn't make anybody feel better.

Ashton Kutcher

There's no text that can replace a loving touch when someone we love is hurting.

Ashton Kutcher

There's something advantageous about having people underestimate your intellect, insomuch as a lot of things are revealed to you. They assume you don't know what you're talking about, then all of a sudden, you do. And the next thing you know, you have information you wouldn't normally have.

Ashton Kutcher

True luxury is being able to own your time - to be able to take a walk, sit on your porch, read the paper, not take the call, not be compelled by obligation.

Ashton Kutcher

Ultimately there's a dirty secret about the Internet, which is nothing disappears. All these companies have all your information. They have your search history.

Ashton Kutcher

Vulnerability is the essence of romance. It's the art of being uncalculated, the willingness to look foolish, the courage to say, 'This is me, and I'm interested in you enough to show you my flaws with the hope that you may embrace me for all that I am but, more important, all that I am not.'

Ashton Kutcher

We all have that desire for something special, something committed. We all want to be The One.

Ashton Kutcher

We haven't lost romance in the digital age, but we may be neglecting it. In doing so, antiquated art forms are taking on new importance. The power of a handwritten letter is greater than ever. It's personal and deliberate and means more than an e-mail or text ever will.

Ashton Kutcher

We're all living in a casino. It's just Vegas. Everything is on camera. Everything is being recorded. Everything is on audio. The truth is we all have access to everybody else's information.

Ashton Kutcher

Wear a belt! It's an easy way to pull together your outfit. Just be sure to match it to your shoes.

Ashton Kutcher

What I've become good at is bringing things that aren't necessarily mainstream to the mainstream. What I did see on Twitter was a potential for mass publication; it's a mainstream consumer broadcasting device. It transforms customers and companies. You have to be transparent or you fail.

Ashton Kutcher

What I've become good at is bringing things that aren't necessarily mainstream to the mainstream.

Ashton Kutcher

When I was 13, I had my first job with my dad carrying shingles up to the roof. And then I got a job washing dishes at a restaurant. And then I got a job in a grocery store deli. And then I got a job in a factory sweeping Cheerio dust off the ground.

Ashton Kutcher

When I was on the "70s Show,' I had that and I had 'Punk'd' and I had my own production company. That pretty much sealed up all my time.

Ashton Kutcher

When you build characters from the outside in, they become, oftentimes they become like 'Saturday Night Live' characters or they become like caricatures of the character.

Ashton Kutcher

When your wife calls, you have to take it, no matter what you're doing.

Ashton Kutcher

Whether it's being a leading man, making TV shows, being with my family, I've learned a lot.

Ashton Kutcher

Whether you like it or not, the digital age has produced a new format for modern romance, and natural selection may be favoring the quick-thumbed quip peddler over the confident, ice-breaking alpha male.

Ashton Kutcher

Women have a level of outward compassion that a lot of men don't necessarily have. Guys feel as deeply as women, but they don't share it as much.

Ashton Kutcher

You know, I think that romance sort of coincides with effort, so you can fall flat on your face, but as long as you're making a great effort, I think it comes off as romantic.

Ashton Kutcher

You know, photo conversations are replacing verbal conversations. I don't know if that's a bad thing. A photo is worth a thousand words.

Ashton Kutcher

Your best T-shirt should be like your bed; it just feels like you are home when you are in it.

Ashton Kutcher

Your shoes have to match your belt. That's rule number one for guys. You can't put the brown shoes with the black belt. Or a brown belt with a black wristwatch. Just don't do it! Also, I don't like boots with suits. And when you wear sneakers, make sure they go with your shirt.

Ashton Kutcher

This page is intentionally left blank

This page is intentionally left blank

This page is intentionally left blank

This page is intentionally left blank

This page is intentionally left blank

www.ingramcontent.com/pod-product-compliance
Lightning Source LLC
Chambersburg PA
CBHW061805280526
45787CB00003BA/1491